BACKSTAGE
IN PARADISE

ROBIN LINDSAY WILSON

Cinnamon Press
:: small miracles from distinctive voices ::

Published by Cinnamon Press
Meirion House
Tanygrisiau
Blaenau Ffestiniog
Gwynedd, LL41 3SU
www.cinnamonpress.com

ISBN: 978-1-78864-070-1

British Library Cataloguing in Publication Data. A CIP record for this
book can be obtained from the British Library.

Designed and typeset in Palatino by Cinnamon Press. Printed in Poland.

Cover design by Adam Craig.

Cinnamon Press is represented in the UK by Inpress Ltd and in Wales by
the Welsh Books Council.

Acknowledgements

Some of these poems (or early versions) have appeared in the following journals or been listed in the following prizes: *Brittle Star, Decanto, Dream Catcher, Northwords Now, South Magazine, The High Window, The Interpreter's House, The Journal, The Rialto, The Seventh Quarry,* & commended in The Sentinel Poetry Competition 2016; shortlisted for the Liverpool International Poetry & Short Story competition 2014.

Contents

for my brother, Neil

Backstage in Paradise

Naturally Occurring Evidence

on the coldest mornings
snails practise writing
I love you in a cursive
and gluey gothic script

the pavement sparkles
with their faint messages —
it's the most they can do
to communicate opinion

under sterilising lights
in an open-plan hierarchy
of PC office managers —
on a brilliant screen
that shivers with data
and worldwide prattle
my scribbles are dry —
only read by the greedy

to tell you the truth
the snails said it better

Torridon

the wilderness says something
and you are busy listening —
the pitch is sharp with birdcalls
the tone is a monster growl

underfoot the flint slides
until you must move or fall—
so you strive above it all

there should be communion
with moor and lichen rock
but nothing feels like pleasure —
you are an off-day witness
not the imagined conqueror

is this the best view?
is this the best glen?
where's the GPS?
where's the outcrop
no one has stood upon?

suddenly light flares out
behind a boulder storm —
this could transcend
all previous distractions

you take a photograph
to define an epiphany
to prove your measurement
of memory and wonder

then press to send
but there is no signal
no signal for how you feel

Poem for a Blustery Day

when it gusts directionless —
when it buffets your side
and stabs your back —
when it clears the clouds
then drops them black

when the memory of love
is twisted and lifted off
leaving an undefended heart
free to care even less
about the old reasons

step forward not back

when there's rain on your breath
and no marrow in your bones

step forward not back

when there's dirt in your soul
step forward not back
when there's fat on your lips
step forward not back
when you are shapeless
behind cheap clothes
step forward not back

the world wants to play
the world wants to play with you —
it has removed all the corners
so you cannot get away

Parallel Witnesses

the woman who mistook autumn for spring
talked about the sticky horse-chestnut buds
to the man who mistook kindness for hope

they had so many mistakes in common
it was inevitable they would risk a kiss
and fondle each other's non-sequiturs

on the steps of the restored bandstand
he offered ice-cream and May Day shade —
she shivered at his plunging tongue
and he blushed at her slurping sounds

when they were reduced to biscuit cones
they fumbled with bits of torn serviette —
she thought he was imagining her naked
he thought she pictured removing his clothes

later in her over-furnished nurse's flat
she mistook his urgency for passion
and he mistook her clinging arms for love

Landfall

she arrives on a glossy prow
cradling a titanium anchor
to gift the sea more sparkle

her shaven skull is speckled
and scratched by negotiating
spinnakers and coral reefs

striding towards the beach
salt dries on her like jewelry

you see yourself sit up
in her mirrored Ray Bans —
you see your open mouth
you feel your tan turn cold

she speaks a language
too beautiful to understand
you feel its taut authority

her shadow falls on you
and holds you underwater
but you don't mind drowning

on your bubbling last breath
she takes off her sunglasses
and wipes the sweat away

where her eyes should be
is the emptiest blue sky

suddenly you can breathe
suddenly you can stand
and offer the whole world
an alternative to worship

Emotional Intelligence

when this double arch
of cream and red bricks
travels through my body
I feel granules of cement
resist my right to be here

when thistledown brushes
my hand and blows back
without finding inspiration
I feel I should apologise

I'm looking at wallflowers
as if they were witnesses —
as if they knew a secret
I grew up learning to forget

here is my childhood place
where I loved being an orphan
and practised my heartache
on cracks in the garden path
and on the caresses of ants

here is my killing ground —
my abandoned investment
and hour-empty paradise

now pulses of June rain
spin baskets of petunias
and the family man watches
hedges soak with ghosts

the scent of drenched soil
stirs skeins of excitements
in geranium hidden corners
and lifts the hairs on my arms

still an expectation of love

as if this suburban garden
holds everything ready
for some simple promise
that I long to make good
if only to the neighbours

Unreported Misdemeanors

he was a well-read soldier
safeguarding the coffin
of some nameless youth —
as it progressed East
to a city with a war memorial

she was studying a face
in her mock diamond ring
and missing her boyfriend

the only reliable test
of a diamond's worth
is how true it cuts —

she looked at him sharp —
it could slice you in half!

he loosened his shirt neck
and presented his stubble
we should give that a try!

the train screamed mercy —
she offered him a sandwich
he invited her to try again
then asked her back home
to meet his mom and sis

she moved to another seat
opened a movie magazine —
flicked over a perfect blond
stared hard at a bathing-suit

and on both sides of dusk
desperate men in doorways —
handsome in spills of light
and wide-awake women
in see-through nightdresses

longed for something eternal
like the blade of a diamond
or a heavy granite stone
to murder their sacred flame

The Assignation

her tiny fluorescent hands
flutter to remain innocent
and free of his great wrists
as she blushes and giggles
at his mucky icebreakers

she's talking to his frown
safe in the brightest glare
of the dismal Doublet bar —
the furthest spot on earth
from a barman's intervention

a guffaw makes her blink
at his beer-yeast breath
and then his thumbs catch

her hands say yes and no —
they say hope and regret —
like a Kelvin Park butterfly
pulsing and folding back
they never leave him alone

he tries a lover's game —
rules gifted by his father
from a softer-spoken time —
his whisper hugs her neck
and crawls into her mind

you are my winter wings-
you are my diamond wings
take me to higher ground

she has a beat of instinct
to push out the fire-door
when an Abba ringtone
makes her hands ordinary
and incapable of lift-off

The Secret Bourgeoise Intensions Of Mermaids

perfumed mermaids
sit on fish-boxes
with webbed fingers
hidden in soggy laps

there's no breeze
on-shore or off —
nothing moves a tail
in front of low doors
made of driftwood

Mr. Right is expected
when the ship sinks
and the strongest kick
for air and the headland

they will know him
by his blistered lips
and plucky whistling

there is a hidden net
and a covered pit
outside each house

until the yell of dust
and the dull man-thud
opens their scaly eyes
they imagine a future
with a Yankee candle
and a nest-of-tables

no wild surf passion
after the wedding vows —
only a hidden pulse
in tiny atrophying gills
while the baby grows

Desire in the Cheap Seats

smoke entertains him
as foolish chorus girls
lift it to their bosoms
with a scoop of feathers

it pulls a strap out of place
then crosses the limelight
to make him swallow

as it shakes and sways
in the body-heat breeze —
climbing the dead smiles
of half-naked starlets
he wants to applaud

a half turn and a high-kick
sends smoke tumbling
along red velvet aisles
to twist under trouser legs —
flipping loose the buttons
on his swollen crotch

when juddering pink hips
lift his soul with a roar
and drum the male ovation
from the Pit to the Gods
he bursts into tears

as the orchestra moans
falters then beats a pulse —
he stands inside the fug
to shout out his demons

Pompeii

it was up hill all the way
with only Jim's confidence
keeping me from backsliding

unnerved by sunset dogs
and the smell of cat piss
on high green tombs

the forum was re-crossed
without a sideways glance
taking the long way around
to the Villa of Mysteries

Jim's shrug delivered
artists of dirty shadow —
lusty cults of Dionysus

satyrs arrived on walls
with horns and phalluses
— madames taught maids
a life of secret pleasure

I wanted to be aroused
to feel centuries vanish
between summer desire
and ancient ejaculation

but truth had crumbled
around blistered plaster —
love was unrecognisable

we looked at our shoes
until we found a way out
across a field of poppies —
the poppies made us talk

I said red a hundred times
he confessed to wonder

Villa Cimbrone

here is a garden for Wagner
to dream of total theatre
in the geometry of a cypress
and the history of a yew

this is the place for Garbo
to practise her last kiss
and then reject her artistry
for little proofs of trust

under ancient bougainvillea
Japanese women in gloves
remove their surgical masks
for a taste of salted caramel

a dancing bronze Bacchus
is stuck between lechery
and a wrong-footed lurch
into middle-age and comedy

I play at love and spontaneity
as if I was outside of history
and didn't long for ice-cream

Rehearsing Humanity

In this makeshift theatre
we rehearse similarities
and improvise the rules
of a long-term friendship.

The skylight midsummer
blesses other narratives
with blazing grubby frocks,
golden half-broken props,
scepters of light-shaft dust.

We grab cloaks and crowns,
grip papier-mâché swords
and shout mock defiance
behind cardboard shields.

The sunlight switches on.
I am the naive stage-king
and you are a wily servant
advising me to pay the army.
The sunlight switches off —
you are the snake emperor
and I am the eagle brother
who insists upon reform.

Cruel things prompt giggles —
in your hair a peacock plume,
in my hand a vial of poison.

Imagination doubts itself,
we collapse with apologies
for tales outside ourselves,
for exaggerations and tests
of right and wrong and good.

Rags pack into plastic bags.
We leave for a lesser world
taking our victories with us.

First Friend

If you hit him with a rock
he would clang real good
and dent shiny like a can
of kerosene. If you held him
under water he would glug
and bubble deep then rise
with a glissando of surprise.
His words click like marbles
or snooker balls. If you left him
because the beach went dark
he would sing love songs
to the silos and the waves.
If you lit him with a match
he would burn steady with
a clear blue flame. He laughs
like rainwater on a cattle trough.
If you threw him from a cliff
he would break clean like
alabaster. Both pieces a right
weight and the edge whiter
to make you think right.
Either half could split your life.

Wasted

I slept
those two times the economy surged
and your backyard gathered a generation
addicted to cappuccino and computer games

you can't expect me to waste my life
every time you send a party invitation

I enjoyed three summers on my mattress
mismatched with Percy Bysshe Shelly
Marvel Comics and idiot Tarot cards

crippled drum-beats instead of sunlight —
a shrill harmonica replacing parents
comparing brother Philip's slick career
to my long joyless marriage with sleep

I could direct a foreign language film —
the way this room tips shadow from my head
and coasts into a flickering afternoon
without food — a naked girl — or wanting

because nothing that crossed my mind
ever made me big stock-market money
doesn't mean the empty sky was wasted
or your drunken barbecue was news

Toon Tours

show-off cartoon crows
on a cheeky beach-towel
flip-flap a salty balcony
challenging Marvel heroes
on damp pants and shirts

on other concrete terraces
thumping tourist hearts
jump from sweaty chests
for giant ice-cream cones
then elastic-snap in place

you are dancing on spray
with a splintered surfboard
jamming open the red jaws
of a perplexed white shark

behind the bike-hire shed
a fang-mouthed bulldog
on an over-strained chain
chokes a centimetre short
of your plump backside

you run against a backdrop
of overstated consequences
and a loop of beach-bars
chased by mice in bedsheets —
their elongated shadows
gaining on your footsteps

your feet burst into flames
and burn like matchsticks —
rocket you above the earth
then drop you back home
with a soot blackened face

now is real time and physics
now is a meantime bore —
you Google the holiday world
for two simple dimensions
where you pay for temptation
with an anvil flattened head

away from the width of the sea
away from the length of sunlight
loving in three dimensions
takes more than animation
and makes you far too sore
to do anything but escape

Alternatives

we make faces at headlights
until they flare and swerve —
we lob stones at exhaust pipes —
personalised number plates —
anything with *baby on board*

let's make our own porno films
we can do it on our phones
and post it around the world

let's start saving for a waterbed
you can order it from Amazon —
I want a pedigree Labrador pup
and a bedroom of our own

we could astonish the seaside
or the house where you were born
where the curtains look the same
but the garden gnomes have gone —
let's get pissed to forget the tide
and chew gum like film stars

let's shoplift for new clothes
or steal your mum's credit card
and max it out on Breezers —
I like pineapple and peach
you love that shot of coconut
cool on your smoker's cough

let's climb the graveyard wall
to break the wings off angels
kick those praying hands apart
and rap all night like Jay-Z
until the dawn burns our souls

Tour de Force

the lopsided crown is stiff
from whisky sweat gone cold —
he's been touring too long
as a king who forgets his lines
but is sure about his fists

the bush audience scratches —
they belch lager insults
throw cans of frothing piss
at anything exaggerated
with no intention to miss

who in this dried dag
of a sheep shagger's brothel
has ever killed a man?

the cheer is spontaneous
drunken and dangerous —
the crowd entertains itself
until his left eye finds faces
and his lofty verse returns

things bad begun

their shouts are divided
some sshhh new threats
as the chirrup of crickets
begins to direct attention

things bad begun
make strong themselves by ill

later when the king lurches
looking for his dropped sword
their belief becomes pity

then terror when he finds it

The Big Time

eyebrows arch with innuendo —
behind his face is an opera plot
of confusion and surprise

he has Don Giovanni's arrogance
but with wet lips unable to close
and a nose without a septum

when he exits for champagne
he's a blond Maria Callas
before she made her come back —
he's a scream behind a curtain
and porcelain being thrown

he returns with a fizzing coffee-mug
and a broken conductor's cane —
he's an octave higher than Tosca
teetering upon her dizzy parapet
as he waves to sponsors in gilded boxes

he would cut his public dead
despite their clamour for a curtain call
if his imitation of tragedy
convinced him he was loved
by anyone but publicists

Brecht In La-La Land

Brecht does not speak English
Laughton doesn't speak German

but J. Edgar has his ear to the wall
just in case they don't like movies

the self-important conspirators
act out heavy-handed stories
about science betrayal and heresy

they both want to be Galileo

here between chrome ashtrays
and Props Dept. furnishings
the air-conditioned gestures
and long-hand political irony
is blue pencilled and typed
for Hollywood's war effort

to the sun it does not matter
that Galileo is coward or hero
or damned by the playwright
who rescued and rewrote him

it's the fat guy's graceful hand
it's the foreigner's listening chin —
the movie star's rubber face
risking a capitalist suggestion

it's the exile's offered banjo song
under a portrait of Mr. Chaplin

stinking writer and homosexual
circle in doubt and come to rest

they smoke cigars and laugh
dismissing remake after remake
until they create the perfect
'what if?' in any language

Compound Memory

an Italian squats by a monkey
and forces a peeled orange
into its swollen purple lips

on the frozen cobblestones
a schoolboy's grey stick legs
poke through the vent of a coat

the conductor is in shock
his voice repeats to the police
the dates of each complaint —
his urgent pleas for repairs

the crowd push the street-car
back onto its buckled tracks —
Stanislavsky grins ear to ear

it's a long way to the theatre
trying to remember the details
of a miniature fez and torn shoes

before the house-lights dim
he glues on his moustache
— alters the angle of his hat

the circumstances of the play
require self-pity and remorse —
a landowner's astonishment
when his orchard is sold

in the wings he remembers
a monkey with grey legs
covered by an overcoat
and a boy with purple lips

despite the mistaken memory
his performance will ring true

Travelling Theatre

the entertainers are cursed
by clicks of chewing gum
and the background radiation
of tablets and cellphones

every story told is a shoot-out —
everything the stunt-boy does
is surprise surprise surprise

below the buckskin swagger
a quorum of timid shadows
fills with derisive laughter —
the sound swirls then returns
with warmth and a real grin

one soul tips into another

the actors increase in height
and grow more handsome
to play a single character

this drunk I am playing now
is not the callow husband
stuttering his wedding vows
to the girl with no perfume —
this flint-eyed Scotsman
is the outsider you once were
before you compromised
with Cava bubbles and rain
decking and a trampoline

the come-back audience roars
as if history was someone else

Open to Influence

beyond a torn screen-door
a naked sixty-watt bulb
provokes lazy daughters
full of sluttish oestrogen
with their glaring bare legs
to come onto the porch
and squash cockroaches

the harvest moon vanishes
and returns with tornadoes —
hot gusts of oily ladybirds
and a heady scent of musk
to torment the neighbourhood

the art teacher wakes up —
she cannot explain chiaroscuro
or how to make love last

she drives on weak sedatives
looking for reasons to blink —
a horny cowboy to pick up
or a motorbike to sideswipe —
things to change her luck

the radio can't find a station
it's all hissing kingsnakes
when she hits the neon sign
and spins across the highway

no real damage done
only a dent in the sunrise
and the beginning of tears
when grasshoppers thump
through the side windows
onto her cold leatherette
and her child's paint-box

Piet Mondrian's Victory

Between the boogie and the woogie
a grateful refugee flicks on the lights
and tries to blind his guilt with glare.

Despite a ribbon of Broadway billboards
the spit and grit of religion remains
until every block is a hymn of praise
to his belief in the god of geometry.

The horizon is always a starting place,
it divides the world into judgments
and creates a line across emptiness
like a Zeeland wall against high tide.

On polder basins and reclaimed land
he builds the foundation of a jazz city.
Electric yellow and red filaments flicker
around the edges of his Puritanism.

When his faith is exhausted on pretzels
and showgirls on The Great White Way
something like acceptance or real life
props a bottle of beer on his shoulder
and calls a cab to Jelly Roll him home.

Ghost Writer

I traded in petty violence and robbery —
a fish-knife or a bottle of bootleg whisky
while I drifted across archipelagoes
trying to avoid blue-eyed missionaries

I met him plucking a scrawny chicken —
bunches of feathers finding the wake
and twirling into leathery mangroves
as he told me a Scottish ghost story

I was his amanuensis on a coral island
when he ran out of cigars and invention
and between coughing bouts of phlegm
and strings of blood gathered into leaves
I wrote self-recriminations to his debtors
and witty begging letters to loved ones

I moved him nearer the steamboat dock
where I could win at most card games
and he could seduce the island girls
with translations of his romantic poetry

but he fought with the shipping agents —
he quarreled with Baptists from America
until complaints reached the governor
who sent militia men to smash his still
and topple his pornographic sculpture

when his wounds turned phosphorus
I rowed him out past the inner reef
and stretchered him onto a sampan
heading in the direction of his family

instead of choking out a brief farewell
we sang sea shanties across the lagoon
and swigged at a demijohn of bandy

when I arrived back at the palm trees
and the shack I saved from the typhoon
I did nothing but stare at the breakers
until I matched them bellow for bellow

I watched the wind finger his manuscript —
fling it page by page towards the rocks
when it was almost gone I roused myself —
now I have bound it with my bootlaces
and replaced his signature on the cover

Trophies

the terrified white horse
rearing on the highway
made us wish out loud
our friends were here
to calibrate our shock

the rock-tomb goats
ripping down unripe figs
were something authentic
we could not approach

but a tortoise scratching
on the parched mosaic
of a half-excavated villa
windmilled the static air
when I turned him snug
against my sweat-patch chest
for a smiling trophy-shot

I wanted a tiny sacrifice —
a lacquered shell to crack —
a neck to own and twist
my will upon the world

scaly toes at the seams
of my wrong intentions
levered my conscience
and ripped my T shirt

after the camera clicked
the prize spasmed freefall
onto a game of naked athletes
with their genitals chiseled
blank by fearful Christians

giving the beast its liberty
restored my false ideas
of birth-right compassion

Herculaneum

from the tourist traps
with their resin replicas
of horny Roman deities
the future has receded
like the Tyrrhenian sea

now is only 2,000 years
of the present tense
and cicada whitenoise

where's the progress here?

we go down to the baths
past the city centre brothel
to Perspex covered graffiti
that slanders a celebrity
from a gladiator school

the sleek telephone wires
and the commuter trains
assume needs have changed
in dreams and pockets

between tiny rooms with tv
and tiny rooms with frescos
the measurements match

but I can tell the difference
between below and above
the scar of excavation

in my neighbourhood
the chairs
the bed
and the stove

are all on credit cards
owned by the servants

Judgment Day

The warty High Court judge
and the snivelling defendant
fight each other's prejudices
in the Court of Last Chances.

The criminal trusts his insults —
he can give as good as he gets
and stand up to posh blokes.

The judge has no faith in men
he believes in original sin —
in near-set eyes, weak chins,
low foreheads, red hair —
eyebrows too close together.

His blunt brimstone profile
is an Old Testament threat
to jurors inclined to mercy.

The thief steals innocence —
hides it in false statements
and the power of absolutes.

The judge robs justice
and blames the godless
for each illegal precedent.

Both believe in appearances
and the punishment of pride.

The Last Supper

in the beginning
the wine was blood
the bread was flesh

the shock of it
teaching generosity
to anyone hungry

when hands needed —
wheat was harvested —
when mouths wanted
the oven was lit

but the dry crumbs
falling from the table
were confiscated
by men in scarlet robes —
the miracle confined
beyond gilt banisters
and baroque gates

the transubstantiation
hidden behind a crystal
set in gold filigree

the faces of the rock
dimmed with incense —
quartz turned opaque
requiring absolute faith
to conjure it clear

when the holy relic
crumbled into filth
and was neither food
nor immaculate flesh —
no facet of expectation
could turn the trick

Judging by Appearances

Remember the invented girl
you created in front of a mirror
to discover you were trapped
between a public sheet of ice
and a private stream of lava?

She still needs to be popular.

You copied your best friend's
habit of sucking her teeth
and spying under her fringe
until your indifferent parents
discussed a sudden beauty
and rewarded your imitation
with chocolate and attention.

Other friends lent you wisdom
and charming idiosyncrasies —
they loved the easy originality
you borrowed from a cousin
who sounded high and careless.

An old friend looks concerned
but you are already forging
that authentic caring frown
that will make her confess
she imitated your disaffection
and stole your wistful smile.

P.C. Plod's Whistle

rabbits with tennis rackets —
mice having afternoon tea —
ducks shopping in Harrods

the best minds surrender
to comfortable daytime TV

the policeman's whistle
is stolen by a giant bear
in a tight rainbow jumper

both know there is no law
except jam and honey cake
and there is no point in life
without infantile pleasure

you gorge on sugar cubes
drink sugar through a straw
and steal sugar kisses

cartoons and false danger
isolate the present tense —
you make the future cruel
but without any real tears

Creating a Family

when my son reached puberty
I was painting the Mona Lisa —
when my wife slipped into a coma
I was writing *War and Peace* —
when my daughter got married
I was composing The Rite of Spring

when I retired from public life
my family painted a bull's eye —
pinned it secretly to my back

I was oblivious to the verdict
until I heard the first gun shot

Torturer

crooked blasts of light
were stapled helplessly
to the corridor wall

the torturer blinked
loosened his top button
broke into a whistle

undid his Topshop tie
draped it over his shoulder

and on his way to lunch
through the swing doors
recognised a merciful God

lighting his long stride
to the Chef's Special

Story Tellers

for Otto Dix

When nihilism was a shimmy
of sweat-drunk black-jazz,
I was ready to lose my faith
in the person on the corner
with crutches and a monkey.

When Hitler stood at his seat
and took the whole scene in,
slaves hid in returns of scenery
handing half-finished props
to line-lost wide-eyed actors.
Behind the prompt-desk dials
I sketched every kind of dark.

The entertainment was cruel
and its punch-line was hatred.
The audience stood to clap
and I almost broke my promise
to the foreign doctor upstairs
peering through the floorboards —
his eyes without an anesthetic.

For a postponement of terror
I shared each ghost-spasm
between the swinging light-bulb
and the blood-stained door
until every lie and confession
felt at home in my heart.

And I almost lost my trust
in sergeants and pick-pockets
who understood deception
but made it serve their skill
at robbing life from death.
And I almost lost my pity
listening to the blank refugee
falsify his name and family
until I realised my only talent
was to validate his memory.

The Private Lives of Slaves

we picked your grapes
we poured your wine
we cleaned your rooms
we spread our flesh
upon white sheets
and waited for your jerk
to break the porcelain

but when you ordered
us to beat our drums
when you ordered us
to make a song
when you ordered us
to dance with joy —
we could not sing
we could not leap
nor beat our drums

so we invented lies
misdirecting your desire
to younger bodies

until a secret signal —
a secret gathering
in a secret place
where we could sing
where we could dance
and beat our drums
without a lie
without an order

there we stood
completely silent
completely still
until the grey dawn
dispersed us to duties
and to our masters
because no command came

After Dinner Speakers

every verdict in the world
was gathered secretly
behind the barbed-wire
and machinegun towers
of a held breath in Poland

we shrugged at the obvious
burst dolls and suitcases —
we imagined naked men
heading for the showers
then fled from imagination

back in a garden hotel
we defended curiosity
to well-fed dinner guests
who predicted shock
and medical treatment
for sick little tendencies

our photos were evidence —
stiff unsmiling visitors
in front of dusty atrocities

those buckled images
wrapped in festive scarves
looked like off-duty officers
posing for family at home
who still believed in orders
and the mastery of one race

Six Strokes

he narrows his eyes
presses his lips together

he dips the brush
into the paint pot
without touching the sides

left to right stroke
45 degrees down from left stroke
45 degrees down from right stroke

he makes a triangle

he breathes in
but his lips stay tight —
pushes in the brush
it goes too deep

left to right stroke
(cutting off the tip)
45 degrees up from left stroke
(that's the difficult bit)
45 degrees from right stroke

he makes a second triangle
overlapping the first

he breathes out
his lips relax —
everyone forgives
the drips on the pavement

easier than he imagined
making a yellow star

not difficult at all
to do the next one

Ambition

desert raw companions —
survivors without smiles
ask directions to the sea

I describe an estuary
and a strategy for dhows
if they will follow my lead
and pay for my services

they are mirage fooled
but the journey is good
when we turn mist to water
and water into sweet tea

they say I can be trusted
but when transport arrives
I charge double for petrol
sell out-of-date medicine
offer guns and ammunition
to the fat thug in charge

why become a refugee —
why trade boredom in the sun
for boredom in the shade
when war is a dust-devil
bringing good business?

The Revelation Paradox

all the epiphanies
between conflicting orders
unsighted mortar shells
and falling uniforms

are shadow cast
into blades of browning grass
or staring up
at another world
moving through the trees

between the screams
is your slow-motion desire
to be unique
to continue to be unique

screams for mamma
screams for god
wordless screams

and so quiet without birds

it feels like openness
it feels like the divine
it feels like a signal
with the nouns missing

it is impersonal —
just four thousand years of warfare
two thousand million combatants
all dreaming of a connection
to the real world

Curves

doctrine kept you unscathed
when friends disappeared
in the backs of black vans
and intellectuals starved

under Mucha chandeliers
you stared straight ahead
at the enemies of big ideas

you wanted grappling hooks
of first principles and certainty
to tumble every pink curve
into dust motes and history
but ideology changed sides
and comrades cut each other
with gestures and cyphers
before the committee vote

you survived the sham trials
to join the first night crowd
taking their red velvet seats
under twisting plaster vines
creating breasts and bellies
from fronds and pale voids

it is right angled geometry
that bulldozers tore down
and rearranged into towers
only good for the infill core
not the face of restoration
needed to bring the tourists
who circle your scarlet flag
and listen to you celebrate
the history of art nouveau

The Goodnight Diary

I dress to go to bed
in a white trim-fit shirt
a narrow black silk tie
grey pleated trousers
a six-button waistcoat
a wool blend blazer
black oxford shoes
and a gun in my pocket
to shoot at the bogyman

the bed is extra hard
but I am not restless

I wake without trouble
at precisely six am —
no dent on my pillow
sheets firmly in place
no crease on my suit
no dream to take to work —
just a gun in my pocket
to shoot at the bogyman

The Theatre of Fear

the actor in the wings
is afraid of telling a lie —
audiences want truth

he can only pretend

the audience is afraid
of trusting in make-believe
and stupid coincidence
when only mirrors matter

he can only imitate

the actor enters with energy —
he remembers the first word
and hopes the next is ready

he can only bluff

the audience is afraid of tricks
written by angry nobodies
too clever to tell a story

he can only play

applause relieves everyone —
the illusion of truth telling
has survived false scrutiny

he can only fool

applause confirms the end
of imagination and danger
and the start of a real life
believing mirrors are true

he can only deceive

City Love

a biting evening frost
defines the art gallery
with triple skeins of breath
until the building dissolves
and reassembles itself
as a palace from Arabia

I want to be thin
and wear heavy boots
on a dark road with rain

I want to lavish friendship
on shut-down trees
and fiery young faces
outside of takeaways

my skeleton is running
through an ancient smell
hidden in woman's coats
towards the great darkness
at the centre of the city

I do not want a lover —
I want a tough crowd
flirting with punches —
returning the faint hope
of elation inside winter

the Kelvingrove Gallery
rejects its foundations
soft towers and turrets
stretch and levitate

I want to hitch a ride
past graffiti shadows
into the staring moon
and out the other side

I want my breath back
to sing a new love song
to the night-club queues
and the drunken students
who dance in the gutters
and call the place home

Buddhism for Dummies

imagine an ocean inside a cloud
imagine a tree growing upside down
imagine the family inside an orphan

imagine the kiss of a basking shark
imagine birds refusing to land
imagine a beggar being born

imagine a dream inside a chrysalis
imagine desire between your parents
imagine your child loading a gun

imagine never going back home
imagine insects feeling pain
imagine the start of space-time

give it all to an evil woman
then imagine her doing good
because she imagines forgiveness

The Way We Are Now

we listen to the small talk
of sea-loch and shore —
we cannot help but smile
when the conversation
sounds like we do now

the consonants click
pebble against pebble —
our noises are precise
vowels stay and rinse
the silt from friendship

we journey to the point —
to the broken crab shells
turning green in the tide
and launch our chatter
of complaint and fear
onto a fluster of waves
and an apology of blue

crunching stones speak
of certainties in the future

the microscopic spill
of death and desiccation
tell us a different story

we look across the loch
and lapse into silence

Tests of Friendship

we should have a frozen cliff —
a strand of frayed nylon rope
and an ice-axe working loose

we should have desert sand —
a bullet-holed water-canteen
and camels unable to stand

I should have a wound —
you should be a prostitute —
one of us becoming kind

I should have a kingdom —
you should have a sword —
both throwing them away

I should be broken down —
you should have a pickup truck —
the future — an open road

do you feel adventurous?

perhaps another time —
when I am on holiday
and your schedule is clear

the ocean welcomes us —
the sunlight says it all

you have a mobile phone
I have an e-mail address

we could easily stay in touch

Loss in Black and White

On Ayrshire's long solemn beaches
I turn away from sea-lion litterbins,
snaking Go-Cart lanes of reeking tires
and Aladdin's tin amusement arcade
to look at a tract of apologetic water.

My childhood is dead and I am back
to grieve beside an ice-cream van
where a cloud island on the horizon
reminds lovers of what they wanted.

I grew up in giant Art Deco cinemas
where I practised every fascination
sitting under a sacred oculus of light.
On Saturdays Hollywood projected
its flicker of romance and fantasy
from the Heads of Ayr to the Holy Isle.

From his hidden base on Goat Fell
Johnny Weissmuller fought heroic battles
against Nazis and plasticine dinosaurs
and swung liana to liana to Lamlash
where he spooked the ivory hunters
and socked them clean to Whiting Bay.

King Kong bit the heads off cannibals,
beating his chest at sharpened sticks
to rescue the screams of Fay Ray.
Fay now has a gorilla neck tattoo
and challenges definitions of beauty.

The concrete beaches are empty
of good and bad and certainty
I feel like I fought the wrong cause
and lurch to the pub like a monkey.

The Cost of Popular Entertainment

the ringmaster lost his whip —
the lion tamer was mauled —
the sword-swallower choked

abandoned by the bearded lady
and a family of contortionists
only the acrobat and the clown
spent the night under canvas
entertaining their alternatives

the tumbler told silly jokes
to the hard-of-hearing clown —
the clown did summersaults
for the old arthritic acrobat

they swigged sweet sherry
to mourn lost colleagues
and their death of purpose

but the clown awoke laughing
in his coffin shaped bed
remembering a punch-line

in a dream of leaping
the athlete spun high
to alight upon a tinsel star

flitting to another country
in a profit-share troupe
of much younger has-beens
they chatted at run-offs
stepped out of sequins
and unzipped torn fat-suits

they never swapped roles
or confused an audience
about who made the jokes
and who took the risks
or whether skill mattered
in all the little doomsdays
screened across the world

they smiled and bowed —
being born for applause
until the big-top came down

Osmosis

park the car in a rectangle
deaf to the swearing boys
blind to the used condoms
until we find blown sand
and a negative of the sea

hardly worth the petrol
when it's undemonstrative

we look pregnant and sweat
like cheese in these anoraks
happy walking windward
sharing scraps of Kleenex

we're expanding with ozone —
our largess hurts like salt
we are identical in respect
for each other's company

our conversation is a search
for more than a dowdy beach
littered with scratched glass
and embossed crab shells

we remember continents —
larger tides and bluer seas
and diagnose our craving
for this sketch of a coast

we talk of rich schooldays
and balancing equations
I remember the formula
for childhood osmosis —
you remember it differently

listen
our conversation swells the sea

In the Palace of Varieties

Adolescents in cloth caps
cling to rearing gilt balconies
giddy as they ride the matinee.
Office boys whistle, stamp,
hiss and blow lewd kisses.

Lime-light burns a narrative,
of obvious set-up, side-step,
and ventriloquist's gag-line.

Pale message-boy Cupids
have throbbing fevered brows.
In the back rows of the Gods,
they love all kinds of ruddy flesh
as long as it giggles and sweats
and drips dangerous hormones.

With stiff new boots and buttons,
they leer at yesterday's starlet
in her port stained baby-smock.

She can't remember the words —
is it Humpy Umpy Umpy Ay
or Umpty Umpty Humpty Ay?

The players cat-call obscenities
as she tugs at shoulder straps,
lets them hang for an eternity
then turns to flash her arse.

There are no velvet curtain calls
only the pennies thrown hard,
with a yell of mock infatuation
until the singer sees her blood
just as young as it used to be.

The Dissipation of Pinocchio

in a yachtsman's club tie
and Armani melancholy
he props up the oak bar
and flirts with widows
in their last blond rinse

one women curls his hair
with nicotine fingertips —
one pays for a Martini —
then taps his forehead
for deathwatch beetles

he was famous once
before his balls dropped
but now he plays the fool
for a lady's hot breath
and a touch of breasts

he retrieves old strings
from his top blazer pocket
with liver-spotted hands —
dangles them over his head
then does a puppet dance
to mock his old restraints

he boasts of other abilities
if he tells a little white lie
with a hobgoblin smirk
and a leer at his flies

the men in the crowd
are uneasy with fairytales
outside they beat him
until his head is bloody
and his nose is a splinter

now he feels like a real boy

The True Story of Romeo and Rosaline

Romeo is in love with Rosaline at the beginning of Shakespeare's
Romeo and Juliet... What if...?

he's in love with adolescence —
he's in love with his mates
who ridicule his love of love —
his infatuation with Rosaline

it's pumping swords in scabbards —
groin thrusts and knob gags
while they dry hump his back
and he half sneers/half blushes

Rosaline plays the long game —
it takes time and absence
for a silly boy to understand
that his friends want him lewd
and as ugly as themselves

slowly she teaches him respect
before allowing wedding vows
and when she loses self control
she finally has a man in Romeo

of course a healthy girl is born —
there are years of sleepless nights
and tired days of goo-goo talk

innuendo drops a stomach —
wantonness grows a silver beard
and pride requires no novelty
other than the hug of a child

grandchildren cling to Romeo's legs
and topple him into make-believe
where he trusts in love at first sight
and muddles the names of roses

Other Matters

for Alison

you do not occur in nature
but you are still natural

I think you are an element
yet to be discovered —
something that cannot age —
that smiles through the night —
a woman with no secrets
on the periodic table

your quiet moonshine
will be a symbol in a box —
a letter with a loop
on a laminated chart
in a future science lab

before the start started —
before everything today —
you had the laws of certainty
ready for my heart

Divine Metaphors

Taken from the 1784 painting:
'The Reverend Robert Walker Skating on Duddingston Loch'
by Sir Henry Raeburn

the ruddy faced Reverend
shows off without friction

he thinks of how the Devil
enjoys himself in winter

his sermon lacks a metaphor

the Devil is like a frozen loch
no — the Devil is like thin ice

the Reverend hugs the edge
tries a half spin with lifted leg

Jesus is like learning to skate —

Jesus is a gush of warm breath —

the Reverend picks up speed
cuts a perfect figure of eight

leaps when he feels Satan
clutching at his fleeing heels

flash wheech whoosh whee!

the Holy Ghost is — God is —

the Reverend Robert Walker
joyful on a single flying skate

Lullaby For A Folk Singer

for Dave

stories do not sleep
stories never sleep
they find you in the dark
and make your hurt sing

it's the first chord you borrowed
because it belonged to you truly
it's the first chorus you shared
when voices recognised their loss
and lifted up their testimony

it's the scale of the betrayal
it's the time that it took
it's the pettiness of history
it's that we haven't changed a bit

did you walk the birks of Aberfeldy?
did you hear the mavis singing?
did you follow Bonnie Dundee?
did you drink a service to your lassie?
are you my ain kind dearie-o?

it's the Floo'rs o' the Forest
falling as the moon stands still

and all the rogues and wantons
passing round the parting glass
cannot sing us back to blooming

the pride that swelled our chests
when we were young chevaliers
is dismissed by winter's breath
that returns no whisper of youth
or prospect of the world's honour

but you can summon company
when you call we will respond
with love songs of our own

stories do not sleep
stories never sleep
they find us in the dark
and make our hurt sing